Norman T. Carrington MA

Brodie's Notes on William Shakespeare's

Twelfth Night

Pan Books London and Sydney

First published by James Brodie Ltd
This edition published 1976 by Pan Books Ltd,
Cavaye Place, London SW10 9PG

7 8 9

© James Brodie Ltd 1974
ISBN 0 330 50006 6
Filmset in Great Britain by
Northumberland Press Ltd, Gateshead, Tyne and Wear
Printed and bound by,
Richard Clay (The Chaucer Press) Ltd, Bungay, Suffolk

Contents

The author and his work 5

The Elizabethan Theatre 8

The text of Shakespeare's plays 11

Plot and structure 12

Setting, atmosphere and style 15

Characters 19

Scene summaries, textual notes and revision questions 30

General questions 63

Line references in these Notes are to the Oxford University Press edition of *Shakespeare: Complete Works*, but as references are also given to particular Acts and Scenes, the Notes may be used with any edition of the play.

To the student

A close reading of the play is the student's primary task,
but it is well worth seeing a performance if possible.
These Notes will help to increase your understanding and
appreciation of the play, and to stimulate *your own* thinking
about it: *they are in no way intended as a substitute* for a
thorough knowledge of the play.

The author and his work

Surprisingly little is known of the life of our greatest dramatist, and the little we can be sure about comes mainly from brief references to him in legal or other formal documents. Though there is no record of Shakespeare's actual birth date, we do know that he was christened William at the market town of Stratford-on-Avon on 26 April 1564. He was the third child of John Shakespeare – variously described as glover, wool dealer, farmer and butcher – and Mary Arden, whose family were prosperous local landowners. However, until the year 1578, when his business began to decline, John Shakespeare was a notable figure in Stratford, and William was probably educated at the local grammar school – where he would have learned the 'small Latin and less Greek' of which the playwright Ben Jonson (1572–1637) accused him. But John Aubrey (1626–97) in his *Brief Lives* (written in the seventeenth century but not published until 1813) says that Shakespeare had 'enough education to become a schoolmaster' – and stated categorically that his father was *not* a butcher.

In 1582, at the age of eighteen, Shakespeare married Anne Hathaway, a woman eight years his senior, who bore him two girls and a boy: Susanna in 1583 and the twins Hamnet and Judith in 1585. He is thought to have left Stratford for London in 1585: there is a tradition (which Aubrey does not deny) that Shakespeare had to flee his native town to avoid prosecution for stealing deer in Sir Thomas Lucy's grounds. But, more to the point, it seems that he left with a band of strolling players, the Queen's Players, who visited Stratford in 1585.

Whether he took his wife and children with him to London is not known, but a pamphlet published in 1592 by a lesser playwright Robert Greene mentions Shakespeare as an actor and playwright. Plague caused the theatres to close in 1593; on their reopening in the following year we know that Shakespeare was by then a member of The Lord Chamberlain's Company (known after the accession of James I as The King's Men). It is probable that he stayed with this company throughout the remainder of his career, writing plays and acting in them in various theatres. His connection with the company must have brought him considerable financial reward, and Shakespeare seems to have been a good businessman as well, for when he retired to Stratford in 1611, aged forty-seven, he was already a fairly wealthy man and a shareholder in two theatres, the Globe and the Blackfriars. He purchased New Place, one of the largest houses in Stratford – where he entertained Ben Jonson and the poet Michael Drayton (1563–1631), and – by the astute purchase of tithes and arable land – he became, in the tradition of his maternal forefathers, a prosperous landowner. He died in Stratford-on-Avon on 23 April 1616, survived by his wife and two daughters.

As an actor Shakespeare does not seem to have been particularly successful; but even in his own day his fame as a dramatist and his personal popularity were great. In 1598 Francis Meres (1565–1647), the writer of critical assessments of playwrights, described Shakespeare as 'the most excellent in both kinds' [i.e. in comedy and in tragedy], and even Ben Jonson, whose dramatic work was in a very different vein, remarks of Shakespeare in *Discoveries* (published posthumously in 1640), 'I lov'd the man and do honour his memory (on this side idolatry) as much as any.' And John Milton (1608–74) wrote in his poem 'l'Allegro' (1632) the often-quoted lines: 'Or sweetest Shakespeare fancy's child/Warble his native woodnotes wild.'

Shakespeare probably began his work as a dramatist by collaborating with others and patching up old plays for his company to revive. His first completely original play is believed to be *Love's Labour's Lost* (?1590), though the date of each play presents a problem: the dates are not given in the First Folio (the first collected edition of his plays, 1623). His first narrative poems, composed during the Plague when the theatres were closed, were *Venus and Adonis* (1593) and *The Rape of Lucrece* (1594). His 154 *Sonnets* were published in 1609 – without Shakespeare's permission, it is said. The first 126 of these intensely personal poems are addressed to a young man, the poet's friend and patron; the remainder to a 'dark lady'. The identity of neither of these two inspirers of the sonnets has been established – nor has it been decided how far the series is autobiographical.

Most of the plays were written for performance in the public playhouses, and were conveniently classified in the First Folio in three groups: comedies, histories and tragedies. But these divisions are too arbitrary – the 'comedies' can contain tragedy, the 'tragedies' moments of mirth, and the 'histories' have aspects of both tragedy and comedy.

When, however, the plays are considered chronologically they fall naturally into four periods. From about **1590–93** Shakespeare was **learning his trade** while patching up existing plays and beginning to write his own: to this period belong *Love's Labour's Lost*, *The Comedy* of *Errors*, *Two Gentlemen of Verona*, the three *Parts* of *Henry VI*, *Romeo and Juliet* and *Richard III*.

From about **1594–1600** was the period of Shakespeare's **greatest development**, when he wrote such plays as *Titus Andronicus*, *A Midsummer Night's Dream*, *The Merchant of Venice*, *The Taming of the Shrew*, the two *Parts* of *Henry IV*, *The Merry Wives of Windsor*, *As You Like It* and *Twelfth Night*.

Despite what we have said above, the period between **1602–08** can be described as that of **the tragedies**, which include *Hamlet*, *Othello*, *King Lear*, *Macbeth* and *Antony and Cleopatra*.

Shakespeare's **final period (1610–13)** includes three romances: *The Tempest*, *Cymbeline* and *The Winter's Tale*; and one historical play, *Henry VIII*.

As for the original productions of these plays, Shakespeare cared little about the dress of his characters – irrespective of place or period, the actors wore the English fashions of his time. And, whatever might be a play's geographical setting, his clowns and lower-class characters were true London cockneys or British country bumpkins – such as would appeal to the gallery in English playhouses.

Since that time, there have been many fashions in 'dressing' the plays: there have been attempts at contemporaneous setting and clothes – in more recent times some of the plays have been produced against stark backgrounds and in modern dress. But today there is a movement towards vaguely 'historical' dress, and (after decades of sonorous, sometimes pompous and often unintelligible speaking of the lines) to a simpler, more naturalistic delivery, such as Shakespeare's original players probably used. But, notwithstanding the many and various innovations over the years, Shakespeare's genius, his lyrical lines and wonderful choice of words, his warmth and his understanding of the human predicament, continue to bring entertainment and enlightenment to people all over the world.

The Elizabethan Theatre

At the time of Shakespeare there were probably not more than five public theatres in the land, all in London, and they were built according to the design of the inn-yards of the period, which had been found marvellously convenient places for the presentation of plays.

The theatre was circular or octagonal in shape. The main part of the auditorium was the large round pit, open to the sky, in which the poorer people *stood* (the 'groundlings'). Encircling this, round the walls, were three balconies, covered on top but not in front (like the 'stands' on a football ground), and containing seats. The price of admission to the pit was one Elizabethan penny, while proportionately higher charges were made for balcony seats, according to their position. When it was wet the performance was postponed until the next day.

The stage was large, jutting far into the pit, and was without scenery and any but the most meagre properties. Hence it made no difference that people stood at the side of the stage as well as in front. The scenery was created in the imagination of the audience by the words of the characters in the play: it was made part of the play, so as not to obtrude and destroy the illusion of reality.

The play went straight on without intervals. Lack of intervals and frequent changes of scene were immaterial when the stage was without scenery, consequently short scenes like the first two scenes of Acts I and II of *Twelfth Night*, are quite common in Elizabethan drama. It should be remembered that on Shakespeare's stage there were no separate scenes *as such*. In the early part of the present century his plays were presented with elaborate, often spectacular, scenery, and sometimes the audience would become impatient at the constant delays while it was being changed. At the present time there is a return to a simple stage setting, in keeping with that of Shakespeare's day, as for instance, at the Royal Shakespeare Theatre, Stratford-on-Avon. There is good reason to believe that when they were first produced the plays took considerably less time than they do today. The Prologue to *Romeo and Juliet*, for instance, refers to 'the two hours' traffic of our stage'.

The end of a scene was frequently marked by rhyming lines, as at the end of Act I, Scenes 1, 2, 4 and 5. Just as the scenery had to be *put into* the words of the play, so had entrances and exits to be arranged as *part of* the play. In a modern play an actor can get into position before

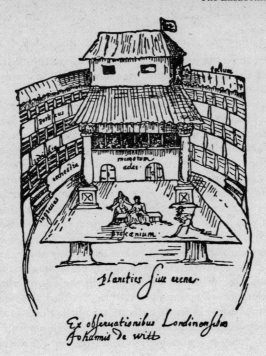

the rise of the curtain, but on the open stage it would seem artificial if
he walked on and then started his first speech, or finished the scene and
then walked off. Such endings as I,1 'Away before me'; 2, 'Lead me on',
clear the stage and at the same time fit in perfectly naturally with the
action of the play. It follows that dead bodies always had to be carried
off the stage in the action of the play.

It was not unknown for the stage floor to be equipped with a trap-
door for the sudden appearance and disappearance of ghosts and
spirits, and some theatres had a flying apparatus by which such could
descend on the stage with the aid of ropes on runners. Under the stage
was the orchestra, a very important feature of the Elizabethan theatre,
and well employed in *Twelfth Night*.

At the back of the stage was a recess 'within', and this was curtained
and could be shut off when desired. This would, no doubt, serve for
the conspirators behind the box-tree in Act II, Sc.5, and for the dark
room in Act IV, Sc.2. Above the recess was a balcony, which served

for an upper room, castle walls and such scenes. This, too, could be curtained off.

The young 'bloods' of the day who fancied themselves actually hired stools round the stage itself. It was a source of continual annoyance to playwrights that actors 'gagged' in order to please these aristocratic playgoers.

By law, no women were allowed to act. Consequently women's parts were taken by boys with unbroken voices. Imagine a boy's rendering of Lady Macbeth or Imogen or Cleopatra! This accounts for the few women's parts in plays of the period, though some were always introduced for the sake of variety. (Among the large cast of *King Henry IV, Part II* only four are women.) It also accounts for the large number of plays where a woman disguises herself as a page boy. It made it much easier for the producer; further, the audience was intrigued by a situation in which a character was pretending to be what he really was.

Plays were not acted in period costume. Thus all Shakespeare's plays were first acted in 'modern dress'. In considering their suitability for presentation in modern dress today, however, it must not be forgotten that the language of the plays fits in with the Elizabethan costume worn by the actors originally. Although there was no scenery, managers spared no expense on the most lavish of costumes.

On days when the theatre was open a flag was flown from the turret, and when the play was about to begin a trumpet was sounded.

The text of Shakespeare's plays

Few readers of Shakespeare realize the difficulties that scholars have had to overcome in order to establish accurate texts of the plays. The First Folio (see p.6), in which, so far as is known, *Twelfth Night* was first printed, contained thirty-six plays. Other collected editions or Folios were published in the seventeenth century, the Third and Fourth Folios containing seven additional plays, none of which, with the exception of *Pericles*, is now thought to be by Shakespeare. Sixteen of the plays had already been published separately as Quartos before 1623, and in the case of some plays, for example, *Hamlet*, more than one Quarto edition exists. Some of these Quartos are almost word for word the same as the texts in the First Folio and were possibly set up from Shakespeare's own manuscript or at least from accurate theatre copies; but others are shortened, inferior versions, possibly 'pirated' editions published by some unauthorized person who had access to theatre copies or parts of them, or who had taken down the plays in shorthand while they were being performed. It is thought that the texts of the First Folio were set up from the good Quartos and from good theatre copies. But these texts must all be compared, printers' mistakes and other interference traced, before a reliable text can be arrived at. The first editor to attempt the problem of the text was Nicholas Rowe (1674–1718), who also divided most of the plays into acts and scenes, supplied place names of the location of each scene, indications of entrances and exits and a list of *dramatis personae*, which are absent from many of the texts in the Quarto and Folio editions. In *Twelfth Night*, however, all the acts and scenes are marked in the First Folio.

While knowledge of the text is important for examination study, it should never be forgotten that the literary and dramatic aspects of the play are more vital.

Plot and structure

Orsino → Olivia. → Viola → Orsino.
Sir Andrew

Plot

Sebastian and Viola, twin brother and sister, of very similar appearance, are rescued from shipwreck on the coast of Illyria, each thinking
the other has been drowned. Viola disguises herself as a page, dressing
in clothes similar to those Sebastian used to wear; and, calling herself
'Cesario', she takes service with Orsino, Duke of Illyria.

Orsino is in love with Olivia, a neighbouring heiress, but she ignores
his proposals; he then sends 'Cesario' to Olivia to see if the 'young man'
can be more successful in furthering his employer's suit. Complications
arise when Viola falls in love with the Duke, and Olivia falls in love
with 'Cesario'.

Olivia's household steward Malvolio had antagonized the other
servants by his overbearing manner; he has also earned the dislike of
Olivia's uncle Sir Toby through his efforts to bring an end to the old
knight's carousals. Maria, Olivia's maid, hatches a conspiracy where-
by Olivia is persuaded that Malvolio is mad, and thus they are able
to have him locked up in a dark room.

Olivia has another suitor besides Orsino – the foolish knight Sir
Andrew, who is buoyed up with false hopes of winning her; and
encouraged to stop at her house by Sir Toby, who then can spend Sir
Andrew's money (on sack). Sir Toby, ever eager for a bit of fun,
persuades Sir Andrew to challenge 'Cesario' to a duel as a rival for
Olivia's love. Sir Toby gives each such a rare account of the other's
bravery and adroitness in fencing that they face one another in fear
and trembling. The duel is broken up by Antonio, who had rescued
Sebastian from drowning and become attached to him, and who now
mistakes Viola for Sebastian. Before explanations can assure him of his
error, Antonio is arrested for an old offence.

Into this mêlée arrives Sebastian, Sir Toby and Sir Andrew, pursuing
'Cesario' to continue the fight, come across Sebastian and get more
than they had bargained for – on two occasions. Olivia marries
Sebastian instead of 'Cesario'. But all the errors arising from mistaken
identity are suddenly made clear on the appearance of Sebastian when
Viola is present and the two are seen together. Olivia adheres to her
marriage with Sebastian; and Viola marries the Duke.

[handwritten: Viola – connecting link for plot + subplot]

Structure

The main plot of *Twelfth Night* is the love story of Olivia, Viola, Orsino and Sebastian. The sub-plot is the conspiracy against Malvolio. Contrast is a fundamental principle of Shakespearean drama. Comic and serious scenes jostle one another through this play (as they do in life), making the comic show up more comic against the serious and the serious more serious against the comic. The student should notice the disposition of the scenes of the main and the sub-plot.

Shakespeare's comic plots usually develop faster than his serious ones. Here, for instance, the success of Maria's conspiracy against Malvolio is assured by Act II, Sc.5.

Plot and sub-plot must not only serve as a foil for each other, they must be well bound together, otherwise the play will be 'broken-backed' and fall apart into two separate plays. In *Twelfth Night* the main and the sub-plot are dovetailed into one another. Two of the chief binding links are the Clown and Maria, who can be equally at home with Orsino or Olivia and Sir Toby and his associates. Viola gets mixed up in both plots and serves as an important connecting link.

The student would do well to make a list of the characters which appear (1) only in the main plot, (2) only in the sub-plot, (3) in both plots.

Note the parallelism in character-studies; Orsino, theatrical, sentimental love; Olivia, theatrical, sentimental grief; Malvolio, theatrical, sentimental vanity. Compare, too, the three studies of 'fools' in the play (see p.29).

[handwritten: Self deceived – Orsino, Olivia, Malvolio]

Mistaken identity in the play

1 In appearance

Viola's disguise as Cesario deceives everyone, more particularly
(a) Orsino (disguised as a man, Viola falls in love with a man),
(b) Olivia (a woman falls in love with a woman disguised as a man).

Sebastian is taken for 'Cesario' by
(a) The Clown,
(b) Sir Andrew and Sir Toby,
(c) Olivia.

[handwritten: 3 fools — Feste – professional fool, Malvolio, Sir Andrew]

'Cesario' is taken for Sebastian by
(a) Antonio,
(b) The Priest.

(c) Olivia and Sir Andrew in Act V also think 'Cesario' is the same 'Cesario' that they had met in Act IV, Sc.1, and Olivia also in Sc.3.

The disguise of women as page boys was a favourite device in Elizabethan drama.

2 In voice
The Clown is taken for 'Sir Topas' by Malvolio.

3 In handwriting
Maria's handwriting is taken for Olivia's by Malvolio.

Antonio's is the only unsuccessful disguise in the play, though it would not appear to be a very complete disguise, apparently consisting in going without his sea-cap (III,4).

1 Appearance
2 Voice
3 Handwriting
} Mistaken Identity

Setting, atmosphere and style

Setting

Most of Shakespeare's plays, apart from the historical ones, are set abroad – a device that can of itself add a certain piquancy. But the local colour of all the plays is that of Elizabethan England, whether the story be one of Italy, Egypt or Denmark, set in whatever age. Nowadays we should demand strict accuracy in scenery, costume and topical references, but then, for playwright and audience alike, the life and spirit of a play mattered more than strict accuracy in local colour. 'It is the spirit which giveth life.' People saw in the drama a reflection of their own life and experience; its appeal was in no way analytical or educational, but human and curiously personal. Shakespeare's characters are men and women before they are Italians or Egyptians.

Further, in those days people were untravelled and uneducated, and anachronisms would not strike a false note in an age more familiar with the stories than with their settings.

And it must be remembered that there was no scenery and no period costume. Incongruities which become apparent beside 'realistic' scenery would not be noticed then, and references to a character's dress must be to something that he was actually wearing on the stage.

Twelfth Night takes place nominally in Illyria (on the east coast of the Adriatic, roughly corresponding to the north of Albania and the south of Yugoslavia), but we are really never far from London. There are references to psalm-singing weavers, ill-reputed tinkers, a 'crowner' (I,5); 'in the south suburbs, at the Elephant' (III,2); the pastimes of bear-baiting (I,3, II,5, III,1) and 'cherry-pit' (III,5). Fashions in dress include cross-gartered stockings (II,5, III,3, 4) and a steward's chain of office (II,3). And Viola humorously gives the cry of the Thames boatmen, 'westward-ho!' (III,1), while the clown refers to a 'pedant that keeps a school i' the church' (III,2). All these were part and parcel of life in Elizabethan England.

Atmosphere

The title of the play allies it with festivity and revelry, and the audience is not disappointed. *Twelfth Night* is easily Shakespeare's most popular comedy, the sunniest and most harmonious. 'It is perhaps too good-natured for comedy,' says Hazlitt. 'It has little satire, and no spleen. It aims at the ludicrous rather than the ridiculous. It makes us laugh at the follies of mankind, not despise them, and still less bear any ill-will towards them.' Shakespeare has a power of viewing each situation without false sentiment, contempt or satire. He has a keen eye for all absurdities, a genuinely comic figure and a genuinely comic situation, not in isolation but forming an integral part in human relations. Wit and humour are the prevailing notes, but there is a serious background which throws the comedy into relief. Olivia has just had a double bereavement, Viola and Sebastian think that they have been bereaved, life holds nothing for the Duke while Olivia's doors are shut fast against him, the heroine faces wounds or death and cannot make known her love, Olivia loves a dream, and Antonio under arrest knows not what penalty awaits him.

But the theme of *As You Like It* still seems to be running in Shakespeare's mind – 'Sweet are the uses of adversity'; and this 'adversity' resolves itself into fun and happiness. In addition to the undercurrent of seriousness, there is a grip of character which increases the value of the play as a picture of human life. It is far from mere buffoonery playing over the surface of life. Shakespeare's art is not bound down by the technical regulations of the schools; he strives to create a form for himself in which he may represent neither comedy nor tragedy alone but human life.

The humour of the play is many-sided. There is humour of

1 Action
e.g. (*a*) The buffoonery of the jolly scenes of carousal.

     (*b*) The garden-scene where Malvolio is 'practising behaviour to his own shadow'.

     (*c*) The mock duel.

2 Dialogue
e.g. (*a*) Wit.

     (*b*) Jests and puns (see section on Style, p.17).

     (*c*) Misuse of words.

3 Resemblance and mistaken identity (see separate treatment, p.13).

4 Character (see individual treatment of characters, pp.19–29).

It is interesting to see how Shakespeare's happy, comedy scenes usually take place in the open air.

Few plays have so much movement on the stage as *Twelfth Night*. There is generally 'something going on'.

Style

There is some beautiful poetry in the play, spoken by Orsino, Viola and Olivia, many of whose speeches are worth memorizing. Viola's in II,4,112 is an example:

> She never told her love,
> But let concealment, like a worm i' the bud,
> Feed on her damask cheek: she pin'd in thought,
> And with a green and yellow melancholy,
> She sat like Patience on a monument,
> Smiling at grief.

The richness and vividness of the imagery should be noted. The similes and metaphors have that sense of surprise and yet of fitness characteristic of genius. Numerous though the similes and metaphors are, there is seldom confusion, as they are usually connected, or naturally combined in one conception – as, for instance, in the Duke's speech to Viola, (II,4,99):

> Alas, their love may be call'd appetite,
> No motion of the liver, but the palate,
> That suffer surfeit, cloyment, and revolt;
> But mine is all as hungry as the sea,
> And can digest as much.

Many expressions in the play – such as 'Patience on a monument' above – have become proverbial, enriching our language. Other notable ones are: at the beginning of the letter dropped for Malvolio, 'Some are born great, some achieve greatness, and some have greatness thrust upon 'em' (II,5); and the Clown's reference to the 'whirligig of time' (V).

The Clown's songs are not just any kind of songs, thrown in merely to have a song or two in the play, they suit the mood of the moment.

There are fashions in literature as in everything else. A pun has been defined as 'the lowest form of wit', but in Elizabethan times punning was extremely popular, indeed, the Clown describes himself as the Lady Olivia's 'corrupter of words'. The Duke and Olivia enjoy puns just as much as the people 'below stairs'. The double meaning is generally quite obvious, but, in cases of difficulty, owing to changes in the language, an explanation is given in the notes.

The normal form of Shakespeare's plays is blank verse. When prose is used it is for a definite purpose.

Prose is invariably used for

1 Comic characters (e.g. the Clown and Sir Toby) and

2 Characters of lower social position (e.g. Maria, Fabian, and Malvolio).

This was a literary convention at a time when literature was aristocratic and the chief characters in plays (as in life) were kings and nobles. Scenes in which the lower orders of society figure are a contrast; these people live on a lower plane of feeling than the main characters, and thereby emphasize the height of the feeling of the main characters, and the contrast in the medium of expression – prose instead of verse – is in perfect keeping.

3 Letters, formal addresses, etc. (e.g. the letters of Maria and Malvolio, II,5 and V,1 respectively).

Prose is pre-dominant in *Twelfth Night*, in fact about two-thirds of the play is in prose, owing to the large number of humorous scenes. Humorous scenes like Act I, Sc.3 and Act II, Sc.5 are entirely in prose. The changes from verse to prose and prose to verse in the various scenes should be carefully studied and reasons for them sought. Note how in Act I, Sc.4 prose is the medium until the servants are 'aloof', and then the Duke and Viola speak in verse. In Act II, Sc.4 Orsino talks with Curio and the Clown in prose, but with Viola in verse. Similarly Olivia talks with Malvolio in prose, but with Viola in verse. In Act I, Sc.5 prose is used until the heightening of the feeling when Olivia unveils. In Act II, Sc.2 Viola speaks in prose to Malvolio, but reveals the innermost workings of her mind and soul in verse, and similarly changes to verse for her soliloquy after the departure of the Clown in Act III, Sc.1. Farther on in the same scene the medium changes to verse again when Sir Toby, Sir Andrew and Malvolio have gone off and Viola and Olivia are left alone, just as verse is interposed for the conversation of Viola and Olivia in Sc.4. In Act IV, Sc.1 Olivia addresses Sir Toby in verse owing to her intense feeling: even Malvolio speaks in verse when he is sufficiently stirred (V).

Shakespeare shows complete mastery of his style and diction. They are equally suited to the dignified scenes of the main plot and the comic scenes of the sub-plot. Further, there are no ups and downs, there is one high level of excellence.

Dramatic irony

The basis of dramatic irony is the difference between the situation as known to the audience and as supposed by the characters of the play or by some of them. Viola's masculine disguise gives opportunities for delightful dramatic irony in *Twelfth Night*. Reference is made to such in the summaries of Act I, Sc.4, p.34, and Act II, Sc.4, p.43. Similarly in Act I, Sc.5 Viola says 'Yet, by the very fangs of malice I swear I am not that I play', and in Act III, Sc.1 occurs the following conversation.

Olivia   I prithee, tell me what thou think'st of me.
Viola   That you do think you are not what you are.
Olivia   If I think so, I think the same of you.
Viola   Then think you right: I am not what I am.

.   .   .   .

Viola   I have one heart, one bosom, and one truth,
           And that no woman has.

The student will readily find other examples.

[handwritten annotation:] This is dramatic irony because the audience knows Viola is not what she appears

Characters

Viola

Our sympathies are absorbed mainly in Viola. 'The great and secret charm of *Twelfth Night*,' says Hazlitt, 'is the character of Viola. Much as we like catches and cakes and ale, there is something that we like better.' Her character is developed fully, and its various features are here set out in tabular form for convenience.

1 Practical. When we first meet Viola and Olivia they have both lost their brothers. Contrast Viola's practical and Olivia's sentimental nature under the blow. Viola realizes that she has to go on living in the world, and she will honour her brother's memory by doing this as well as she can, not by theatrical show.

2 Brisk and businesslike, with a power of quick decision, e.g. on her plan of disguise at the beginning.

3 Accomplished.

> For I can sing,
> And speak to him in many sorts of music.

(This may be one reason why she advances so quickly in the Duke's service.) She has a knowledge of French, and 'takes the wind out of Sir Andrew's sails' by answering him in French when he little expects it.

4 She has not too great a self-confidence and frankly confesses when she is beaten. This is one of the things about her that wins our sympathy. But she does not worry over things that may never happen. She sees no way out of a difficult situation, and so 'Sufficient unto the day is the evil thereof'.

> O Time, thou must untangle this, not I;
> It is too hard a knot for me to untie!

She will not cross the bridge until she comes to it.

5 A strong sense of honour, loyalty and duty. In love with Orsino, she yet does her best for him with Olivia, and does so well that she gains admittance when others had failed to shake Olivia's decision that no more of the Duke's messengers should cross her threshold. She would never dream of double-crossing him.

> I'll do my best
> To woo your lady: – [*Aside*] yet, a barful strife!
> Whoe'er I woo, myself would be his wife.

She is similarly true to Olivia; for instance, she does not let Malvolio into the secret of Olivia's deception of him with regard to the ring (II,2).

6 Imagination to conceive her plan, spirit and resource, heroism, tact and good sense to carry it out. With these qualities she meets each contingency and triumphs over every obstacle.

7 Like the Clown she is 'for all waters' and adapts herself to the mood of those she is with, e.g. Orsino, Olivia, the Clown. She can be dignified before Olivia, and yet turn aside to give Maria a pert repartee, and half in humour and half in scorn refer to her as a 'giant'.

8 In her second interview with Olivia (III,1) she is polite, self-possessed, firm and yet understanding.

9 Though we see her in a man's clothes and hear her masculine exclamations (e.g. 'Westward ho!') we never forget that she is a woman. Her plight in the duel scene nearly causes her to reveal her identity – 'A little thing would make me tell them how much I lack of a man'. If Malvolio and Sir Andrew were fighting in the duel the scene would be pure fun, but because it is Viola it has pathos as well. Occasionally she forgets her disguise, as when she pays Maria back in her own coin – 'No good swabber; I am to hull here a little longer. – Some mollification for your giant, sweet lady' – a thing no gentleman would do.

10 She is as easily gulled by Sir Toby and Fabian as Malvolio, yet we sympathize with her and admire her. The reason is that we do not feel she deserves it.

11 Her sincerity and common sense stand out against Orsino's dreamy speech-making and also against Olivia's loss of self-respect. Whereas Viola 'never told her love', Olivia throws all sense of decorum to the winds with 'Nor wit nor reason can my passion hide'. Viola loves Orsino more perhaps because she, essentially practical, sees the weakness of his nature. A woman's love often goes out where the need is greatest. She is a good judge of character. She reveals her own character and gives Orsino a lesson in true love in the interview between them. We perhaps feel a little disappointed at her marriage destiny, but Viola, tender, sincere and practical, was able, if anyone was able, to rescue Orsino from conceit, sentimentality and speech-making, and make a man of him.

Orsino

We feel no attraction for Orsino, though he was respected by everybody, fond of music and poetry, virtuous, noble:

> Of fresh and stainless youth;
> In voices well divulg'd, free, learn'd and valiant,
> And in dimension and the shape of nature
> A gracious person.

He gives the impression of being considerably older than Viola. When Viola (as Cesario) says that the age of the woman she loves is 'About your years, my lord', his reply is 'Too old, by heaven'. Apart from definite evidence like this, his whole attitude is that of an older man.

He has no patience with 'these most brisk and giddy-paced times' – things are not what they were.

In the first scene we learn that he is dreamy, changeable, moody, 'high-fantastical'. As the Clown says later, 'The tailor make thy doublet of changeable taffeta, for thy mind is very opal'. His love is sentimental, not genuine. The ruling passion of his life is love of himself. His self-conceit has led him into a pose, and he cannot distinguish the pose from the reality. He has wondered what it is like to be in love, he has tried what it is like to be in love, then he has posed to be in love, and finally has become in love, so far as he can tell. Thus his love is a production of his fancy, he is in love with being in love. He seems to relish his love pains, and likes to talk about them as some people do their ailments. Though he sends messenger after messenger to Olivia, it is a long time before it occurs to him to go himself. Had his love been real he could not have kept away from her. He resembles Olivia too much to attract her: his sentimental love matches her sentimental grief.

To such a being life is intolerable without onlookers; he cannot act before empty benches and therefore makes his grief public. He is very fond of the sound of his own voice. He *does* little, but *says* much (contrast Sebastian).

His words are not those of a deep and sincere nature, and we are not impressed when he is able so easily to transfer his affections from Olivia to Viola. As usual, in the re-shuffle at the end he thinks how it affects himself – 'I shall have share in this most happy wreck'. He bestows himself upon Viola as if he were doing her a favour: in his own eyes he is a person worthy to be loved. In our eyes he is quite unworthy of her love, and we feel sorry that she will have to put up with such a man. Orsino is certainly not of the stuff of which heroes are made.

Olivia

We meet Olivia in mourning for her brother. Her grief is not a natural or a healthy grief.

The element itself, till seven years' heat,
Shall not behold her face at ample view;
But, like a cloistress, she will veiled walk,
And water once a day her chamber round
With eye-offending brine: all this to season
A brother's dead love, which she would keep fresh
And lasting in her sad remembrance.

Like Orsino's love her grief is sentimental and theatrical, and she soon forgets all about it the first time a handsome young 'man' crosses her path.

Yet Olivia is a capable woman. Sebastian notices at once how she 'sways her house, commands her followers', 'with such a smooth, discreet, and stable bearing'.

She is a good judge of character. She cannot help but realize Malvolio's efficiency, but at the same time she sees through his self-conceit.

O, you are sick of self-love, Malvolio, and taste with a distempered appetite.

She keeps herself somewhat aloof and has a proper dignity and pride. Perhaps this helps to account for her smooth management of her household. The servants stand in awe of her and are not likely to take liberties. 'My lady' is always in the background of Maria's thoughts, and the Clown knows just how far he can go.

It appears that she has more control over her household than she has over herself. Used to having her own way, when head over heels in love with Viola she cannot brook opposition, and ends by throwing aside all pride, dignity and reserve – 'Nor wit nor reason can my passion hide'.

Hers is a kindly, generous nature, however, with a strain of wit and humour: for example, her first interview with Viola and her good-humoured bantering of the Clown in the same scene. Her kindly concern for Malvolio goes so far as to strengthen him in the belief that she loves him. When the trick that has been played upon him is revealed, she shows no indignation at Malvolio's preposterous idea that she, to whom the Duke paid unsuccessful court, should love a prosy old steward, only sympathy for his wrongs, 'Alas, poor fool, how have they baffled thee!'

Sebastian

We know nothing but what is good about Sebastian. He is an affectionate brother,

A lady, sir, though it was said she much resembled me, was yet of many accounted beautiful: but, though I could not with such estimable wonder over-far believe that, yet thus far will I boldly publish her, – she bore a mind that envy could not but call fair. She is drowned already, sir, with salt water, though I seem to drown her remembrance again with more.

a loyal friend,

Antonio, O my dear Antonio!
How have the hours rack'd and tortur'd me,
Since I have lost thee!

and we put faith in his vow to be a good husband. He is brave enough to face Sir Toby and Sir Andrew together. He is a man of action; he says little and does much. He has not an exaggerated notion of his own capabilities and self-sufficiency – 'His [Antonio's] counsel now would do me golden service'. He makes up his mind quickly, without dilly-dallying, and, having decided that Olivia is offering him a good chance, he there and then accepts her, although he has known her only for some five minutes. Like that of his sister, his plain common-sense makes a strong contrast with the sentimental natures of Olivia and Orsino. We hope that as Viola's practical nature might cure the Duke of his self-conscious sentiment, so would that of her brother cure Olivia of hers.

Malvolio

Malvolio is the most interesting character in the play, irresistibly comic, yet in some respects serious. It is a very big question whether his should be considered a comic part at all.

He is not without good qualities. He is a competent steward, for Olivia 'would not have him miscarry for the half of her dowry'. He does his job well, and Olivia has not to be at the back of him all the time; he shows initiative as well as routine efficiency.

Go you, Malvolio: if it be a suit from the count, I am sick, or not at home; *what you will*, to dismiss it.

When in a quandary Olivia naturally seeks his presence, even if she does not intend to confide in him.

Where is Malvolio? – he is sad and civil.
And suits well for a servant with my fortunes.

These merits are marred by his greatest defect: 'O, you are sick of self-love, Malvolio'. His self-conceit spoils him, 'the best persuaded of himself, so crammed, as he thinks, with excellencies, that it is his grounds of faith that all that look on him love him'. Consequently he cannot manage the other servants without hurting their feelings.

Of all conceited people those conceited with their own virtue are the most dangerous: they are dangerous to morality, because they bring virtue into disrepute. He is a faithful steward, yet he thinks, because he is virtuous, that there should be 'no more cakes and ale'. He sets up his own standard and considers that everyone else should keep to it. Moral vanity is his failure.

Malvolio looks at his own virtues and other people's faults through a magnifying glass. His attack on Sir Toby is not unjustified. The point is that he enjoys delivering it. See his pleasure at the idea of 'calling his officers about him', and 'after a demure travel of regard, telling them I know my place, as I would they should do theirs.' He loves to walk about in stiff dress with a high-handed manner. He enjoys taking back tales too – 'She shall know of it, by this hand'. Similarly he brought Fabian 'out o' favour with my lady about a bear-baiting here'.

He cannot give a ring back without being sour about it.

She returns this ring to you, sir: you might have saved me my pains, to have taken it away yourself . . . If it be worth stooping for, there it lies in your eye; if not, be it his that finds it.

A 'churlish messenger' indeed.

Malvolio has no sense of humour. He takes everything in dead earnest, mistaking 'bird-bolts' for 'cannon bullets'. He is quite blind to the funny side of Sir Toby's merry-making, and unable to see a joke himself calls the Clown a 'barren rascal'. If people are happy they must be doing wrong.

Such a vain man naturally pays much attention to his personal appearance and behaviour. He spends hours 'practising behaviour' and 'jets under his advanced plumes'. In his idea of his own self-importance he builds castles in the air and forgets that he is 'any more than a steward'.

Malvolio apparently has a touch of hypocrisy. Even if we discount Maria's assertion that he is a 'time-pleaser' – coming, as it does, from an enemy – a conscientious Puritan would never have consented to wear 'yellow stockings' or have imagined himself in a 'branched velvet gown'.

In spite of all we cannot help sympathizing with him in his humiliation. But we must not feel too much sympathy for him, and the news that he has caused the imprisonment of the Captain who had befriended Viola counteracts our sympathies at this stage. Yet at the end we feel 'he has been most notoriously abused', and when he vows revenge we half hope that in some way he will get it. As he is conscious of his humiliation we sympathize with him in a way that we do not with Sir Andrew. The humiliation would hurt him much more than the mere fact of being locked in a dark room, which, after all, was bad enough. For one with his notions of his self-importance it would be terrific. Olivia's few kind words, however, may have been a little consolation for his deeply wounded vanity.

The student will find it a great help to collect everything said about Malvolio, but should bear in mind who is the speaker if he wants to form an unbiased opinion of his character. Note particularly Olivia's words to Malvolio in Act I, Sc.5, beginning, 'O, you are sick of self-love, Malvolio', and Maria's account of him after he has left the revellers in Act II, Sc.3.

Sir Toby

We ought not to like this drunken reveller, but we all do. (Contrast Orsino, a 'stainless' character whom we do not like.) He is not the sort of person whom we should care to have as a friend, but he endears himself to our hearts by his irrepressible genial good humour, keen sense of fun, and sociability. By hook or by crook he means to get the most out of life.

He fleeces his so-called 'friend', and keeps the pretence of friendship until the very end, but we have no sympathy with Sir Andrew, who has more money than sense.

Compared with Sir Andrew, Sir Toby is brave and manly; he is quite ready to fight Antonio and Sebastian.

Although he prefers the company of servants because it is more lively, Sir Toby is in no danger of forgetting his rank. 'Bolts and shackles!' he says when Malvolio imagines himself asking for his 'kinsman Toby', and 'Shall this fellow live?' when Malvolio pictures Sir Toby courtesying to him, and so on.

His boisterous practical joking (e.g. the duel) is horse-play compared with Maria's more subtle and intellectual cleverness. To his credit be it said that he shows no touch of jealousy at Maria's skill. He is capable of admiration of greater cleverness than his own.

It is rather ironical that while he is making fun of Malvolio for being duped by Maria, he is himself being affected by her in a different way. She will perhaps try to 'confine' him 'within the modest limits of order'.

Sir Andrew

Sir Andrew is the most amusing of Shakespeare's half-witted country bumpkins. He has no personality. He is Sir Toby's echo in words, his shadow in actions. He echoes Sir Toby word for word.

Sir Toby   An thou let part so, Sir Andrew, would thou mightst never draw sword again.
Sir Andrew An you part so, mistress, I would I might never draw sword again.
Sir Toby   I smell a device.
Sir Andrew I have't in my nose too.
Sir Toby   I could marry this wench for this device.
Sir Andrew So could I too.

The country bumpkin looks up to the town gallant as having all the qualities for a man to admire and follows his lead unquestioningly. Sir Toby is his ideal. Consequently he is easily fooled by Sir Toby, well supported by Maria and the Clown.

All through he never suspects that Sir Toby is cheating him or loses his faith in him. Right at the end he makes excuses for his hero to 'Cesario', 'If he had not been in drink, he would have tickled you othergates than he did', and he feels sure that his wound will be better looked after if it is dressed with Sir Toby's – 'I'll help you, Sir Toby, because we'll be dressed together'. Sympathy would be wasted on him, for he has the imbecile's happy unconsciousness of his imbecility.

It should not be forgotten that Sir Andrew has a sense of his deficiencies, however. He is quick in praising the fooling of Feste, feeling that though (or because) he cannot understand it, it must be something wonderful. Similarly he realizes his lack of vocabulary, '"Odours", "pregnant", and "vouchsafed" – I'll get 'em all three all ready'.

He is a complete coward. 'If he were opened,' says Sir Toby, 'and you find so much blood in his liver as will clog the foot of a flea, I'll eat the rest of the anatomy.' Fabian's words of 'Cesario' may be with truth applied to Sir Andrew, 'A coward, a most devout coward, religious in it'. Shakespeare delineates his cowardice with great fun. Sir Toby describes his antagonist, and Sir Andrew shows his true colours – 'I'll not meddle with him ... Plague on't, an I thought he had been so valiant and so cunning in fence, I'd have seen him damned ere I'd have challenged him'.

Like most cowards he is a bully. When Fabian says that 'Cesario' is a coward, Sir Andrew says, ''Slid, I'll after him again, and beat him'.

The contempt we have for a character of this sort is lost in Shakespeare's fun and frolic.

Regarding Malvolio and Sir Andrew, it is interesting to consider why, when bores in real life are so dull, they can be made interesting in plays.

Maria

Maria, clever and sharp of tongue, is the arch-foe of Malvolio. Through her keen insight into character she is able to exploit his weaknesses, 'gull him into a nay·vord, and make him a common recreation'.

She can be all things to all men, enthusiastic and gay with the revellers, prim and proper before Olivia.

She probably carries out the conspiracy against Malvolio with an eye to pleasing Sir Toby and becoming Lady Belch as much as for the pleasure of befooling Malvolio. The Clown taunts her with setting her cap at Sir Toby – 'If Sir Toby would leave drinking, thou wert as witty a piece of Eve's flesh as any in Illyria', and Sir Toby himself refers to her as 'a beagle, true-bred, and one that adores me'. In any case, she did please him so much that he said he 'could marry this wench for this device', and lost no time in doing so.

Feste, the Clown (Lat. 'festus' = cheerful, gay)

He must observe their mood on whom he jests,
The quality of persons, and the time;
And, like the haggard, check at every feather
That comes before his eye. This is a practice
As full of labour as a wise man's art.

He is not unconscious of his own ability either, and Malvolio's rebuff before Olivia sticks until 'the whirligig of time brings in his revenges'.

He has as great an insight into character as Maria's, and his comments are as shrewd. Like Maria again, his insight into character helps him to adapt himself to his company. He is 'for all waters' by nature and also with an eye for gratuities. He sings the sentimental Duke ballads of 'silly sooth' that dally 'with the innocence of love, like the old age': he joins heartily in the carousals of Sir Toby and Sir Andrew. In each case he humours his company and gets a 'tip'.

All through he has an eye to his own profit and gets all the rewards he can. Viola gives him 'expenses' and he follows up with, 'Would not a pair of these have bred, sir?' He acknowledges Sebastian's 'open hand', but hints that he would not be averse to more.

These wise men, that give fools money, get themselves a good report – *after fourteen years' purchase*.

And to the Duke he says,

But that it would be double-dealing, sir, I would you could make it another . . . Primo, secundo, tertio, is a good play; and the old saying is, the third pays for all: the triplex, sir, is a good tripping measure; or the bells of Saint Bennet, sir, may put you in mind, – one, two, three.

Clever and good-humoured, he loves to take part in a practical joke, e.g. as Sir Topas. We therefore get rather a shock when Sir Andrew and Sir Toby come up with Sebastian (instead of 'Cesario') and blows are struck and the Clown says 'This will I tell my lady straight: I would not be in some of your coats for twopence'. This savours of Malvolio. By nature the Clown does not seem to be a tell-tale. Perhaps it is owing to Sebastian's generous 'tip'.

It is rather curious that the Clown runs away to Orsino's palace for so long, especially in view of his relish of Sir Toby's company. 'My lady will hang thee for thy absence . . . Make your excuse wisely, you were best,' Maria tells him, so he must have stayed as long as he dared. Perhaps he found Olivia's house different since her mourning, and Malvolio about the place would be no attraction.

The Clown is a fool only by profession. The real fools of the play are Sir Andrew and Malvolio, Sir Andrew a 'natural' fool, and Malvolio a 'deep-contemplative idiot'.

Fabian

Fabian is what is known as a good sport. He got into trouble with Olivia 'about a bear-baiting here', and sporting metaphors come naturally into his vocabulary. He is fond of a bit of roguery, and enjoys the hoaxing of Malvolio and Sir Andrew as much as anybody. At the end he tells a chivalrous lie to Olivia in order to protect Maria, saying that he and Sir Toby 'set this device against Malvolio here'. He cannot get over the fact that Maria has written the letter, so he says that 'Maria writ the letter at Sir Toby's great importance'. Olivia could not vent her wrath upon a kinsman in the same way that she could upon a servant, but, in any case, Fabian goes on to break the news that Maria herself is now a relative of Olivia by marriage.

Scene summaries, textual notes and revision questions

Act I

Scene 1

A scene in a play may do one or more of the following.

1 Advance the action.
2 Create an atmosphere.
3 Develop a character.
4 Give dramatic relief, contrast.
5 Make an impression of the flight of time between two other scenes.

This scene gives the situation previous to the beginning of the play. Orsino, Duke of Illyria, is an unsuccessful suitor of the Countess Olivia.

At the outset it also reveals much of Orsino's character. He is fond of music (this is important as one of the reasons for Viola's rapid promotion in his service), changeable, moody and sentimental. He likes to dally with fanciful language.

appetite i.e. for love.
dying fall Diminuendo.
sound i.e. of the wind
quick Full of life.
That In that.
validity Value.
pitch Height. Metaphor from falconry – the height to which a bird soars.
falls into abatement Depreciates.
shapes Ideas.
fancy Love.
alone Pre-eminently.
high fantastical Highly imaginative.
Why . . . have There is a pun on 'hart' and 'heart'. Is it natural that the duke should pun at a moment like this? As a relief to their feelings people often joke at times of great stress.
turn'd . . . me A reference to Actaeon, who was turned into a hart and pursued and torn to pieces by his own hounds for looking on Diana bathing.
fell Cruel.
might not Was not permitted.

her handmaid Notice how casually the 'brains' of the sub-plot is introduced.

element We should say 'elements'.

till ... heat Until the end of seven years. 'Heat' is a noun.

at ample view Openly.

cloistress Nun.

brine i.e. tears, which are salt.

season Preserve. The same word as in 'seasoning'.

A brother's dead love i.e. her love for her brother.

frame Framework.

To As to.

How ... her Dramatic irony. Orsino speaks only too truly, but it is not to be himself whom she loves.

golden shaft Cupid, the god of love, carried two 'shafts' or arrows, the golden to inspire love, the leaden to inspire hate.

else i.e. except for a husband.

liver Then considered the seat of the affections.

fill'd ... perfections Her sweet perfections are filled.

one self king One self-same king, or one king alone.

Scene 2

Viola has been shipwrecked on the coast of Illyria and thinks that her twin brother, Sebastian, has been drowned. Faced by a difficulty, she is not moaning about it, as the Duke is about his difficulty, but taking quick decisions how to meet it. Look at the masterly way she handles the Captain – a tip here, a compliment there, a promise of further consideration if he manages things well. On her decision to serve Duke Orsino rests the tangle of the main plot and the fun of her contact with characters of the sub-plot.

The conversation between Viola and the Captain gives the audience further particulars of the situation before the beginning of the play in a natural, unobtrusive way.

driving Drifting.

Arion When Arion, Greek minstrel and poet, was on a sea voyage returning to Corinth with rich treasure, the crew of the ship captured him and were about to kill him for his treasure. He asked to be allowed to sing one song before he died. This was granted, and Arion suddenly jumped into the sea, to be carried to land on the back of a dolphin fascinated by his music.

The like of him i.e. that he has escaped too.

bred Begotten.

I have heard my father name him Note this remark, it becomes important later on.

He was a bachelor then A casual remark, but having a close connection with the plot.

late Lately.

fresh in murmur The latest rumour.

less i.e. in rank or position.

deliver'd Made known.

Till ... is! Till I had made a good opportunity to make known my rank.

though that The 'that' is redundant.

wall Outside.

close in Enclose.

suits with Agrees with.

shall become the form of my intent I shall decide on.

eunuch Servant.

allow ... service Prove me to be well worth having in his service.

Scene 3

In a typical scene we are introduced to the leading spirits in the sub-plot, which provides the comic relief.

Sir Toby keeps Sir Andrew at Olivia's house, ostensibly to further his suit to Olivia, really to spend his money for him.

cousin Used loosely of any relationship in Elizabethan England. So today a man calls a boy 'son' without any suggestion of the actual relationship.

before excepted Those things which have previously been taken exception to. A legal phrase – 'exceptis excipiendis'.

modest Moderate.

confine Sir Toby takes it as applied to clothes.

straps Tags.

tall Courageous, valiant.

to the purpose To the point.

but a year Only a year.

viol-de-gamboys Sir Toby's rendering of 'viol-da-gamba', the violoncello. 'Gamba' = leg (Ital.) – the instrument is held between the legs.

almost natural i.e. a born fool.

gust Relish. cf. 'gusto'.

substractors Sir Toby means 'detractors'.

coystril A mean, worthless fellow.

parish-top Kept to encourage the peasants to take exercise in cold weather when they were unable to work, and so keep them out of mischief.

Castiliano vulgo An explanation with a Spanish sound, though incorrect and here meaningless. Such phrases were very fashionable after the defeat of the Armada.

What's that? i.e. the meaning of 'accost'. Sir Toby often makes fun of Sir Andrew without his realizing it by taking him in a different sense from what he intends. Maria does so too in the following speeches.

An If.

let part i.e. let *her* part. Notice Sir Andrew's next words to Maria – he cannot think for himself, he is a mere echo.

Marry An oath, referring to the Virgin Mary.

bring ... drink A proverbial phrase ('metaphor') in which a forward maid asked for a kiss and a present. The 'buttery' was the larder, and the 'bar' where the food and drink were served.

It's dry, sir Maria still has Sir Andrew's hand, and a dry hand was supposed to be a sign that the owner was too old for love.

What's your jest? Sir Andrew cannot fathom these double meanings.

barren i.e. of jests.

lackest Needest (in order to sharpen your wits). Sir Toby no doubt feels that he could do with some canary too!

canary Wine from the Canary Islands.

put down i.e. in a combat of wits.

eater of beef The Englishman's love of beef has always been a stock subject of satire.

What is 'pourquoi'? This from the man Sir Toby said spoke 'three or four languages word for word without book'.

fencing, dancing, and bear-baiting All fashionable Elizabethan sports.

Then hadst ... hair A pun on 'tongues' and 'tongs' (for hair-curling).

a housewife i.e. Olivia. Sir Toby kept Sir Andrew at Olivia's house on the pretext of helping him to court her and meanwhile was a parasite upon him.

life in't i.e. promise in your suit.

masques A masque was an entertainment very fashionable at the time, consisting of theatricals and dances. Originally the performers wore masks.

revels Entertainments, such as masques.

kickshawses Trifles.

betters Those more expert than himself.

old Expert, as in the phrase 'an old hand'.

galliard Caper, quick dance.

back-trick A caper backwards.

hid i.e. from Olivia.

Mistress Mall If a reference to 'Moll Cutpurse', an infamous character of the early seventeenth century, this is a later addition, as at the time *Twelfth Night* was written Moll would be only a girl. Valuable pictures in art galleries often have a curtain over them to protect them from dust and light.

coranto Another quick dance.

star That men's natures were influenced by the star under which they were born was a widespread superstition of Elizabethan times.

indifferent, well Fairly well.

stock Stocking.

sides and heart Really Taurus was supposed to govern the neck and throat.

Scene 4

Twelfth Night is a play of love at first sight. The first instance occurs in this scene. Viola, disguised as a page boy under the name of 'Cesario', is sent to plead with Olivia on behalf of the Duke, when we become aware that Viola herself falls in love with her master. This is a complication which increases the suspense of the audience.

The interest of the scene is sharpened by the dramatic irony from remarks which have a subtle secondary significance owing to Viola's disguise as a boy.

This serious, romantic scene follows on the heels of an uproarious scene (see p.9). Contrast throws both into greater relief.

advanced Promoted. Viola's skill in music (see her last speech but one in Sc.2) would be a strong recommendation to the Duke. (Valentine's own promotion may have been hindered by his inability to gain access to Olivia.)

humour Mood, temperament, disposition.

Stand you. Cesario, Thou 'Thou' was a sign of familiarity; 'you' was a formal address.

less but Less than.

spoke Said.

civil bounds Bounds of civility.

unprofited unprofitable.

Say Suppose.

dear Intensifies 'faith'.

attend Listen to. Note the dramatic irony of these words, which turn out to be only too true.

nuncio Messenger.

art a man Have arrived at man's estate.
rubious Red, like a ruby.
pipe Voice, literally throat.
sound Clear.
semblative Like.
part A theatrical term.
constellation Character (owing to planetary influence).
as freely ... thine To call thy lord's fortunes thine as freely as he does
  himself.
barful Full of *bars* or obstacles.

Scene 5

Viola presents the Duke's love-suit to Olivia. Another complication
follows when Olivia falls in love with Viola.
  The first meeting of Viola and Olivia is very important, as so much
follows from it.

1 Olivia falls in love with Viola, producing a whole set of complications ending with her marriage to Sebastian.
2 Olivia is made all the more proof against Orsino's advances.
3 Sir Andrew considers Viola as a rival for Olivia's love, so challenges
'him' to a duel.
4 Olivia forgets her grief.
5 This visit is the cause of a second visit by Viola.

It is significant for the sub-plot that Malvolio earns the enmity of the
Clown, making him only too eager to catch at an opportunity of
'taking him down a peg'.

Make that good Prove it.
lenten i.e. meagre (like Lenten fare).
for turning away, let summer bear it out As for being turned away,
  summer will make it bearable (more than it would be in winter).
gaskins Loose breeches. Maria puns on the word 'points' as meaning
  'buttons' attaching the gaskins to the doublet.
if Sir Toby ... Illyria A hint of another love affair.
You were best It were best for you.
Quinapalus A name invented by the Clown.
madonna My lady.
botcher Mender of clothes.
syllogism Argument.
so Well and good.

Misprision Mistake.

Cucullis non facit monachum 'A cowl does not make a monk'. The fool applies this proverb to his fool's costume.

Dexteriously Dextrously. No doubt the Clown intended the mistake; it is in keeping with his whole humorous bearing.

mouse A term of endearment.

idleness Method of killing time.

no fox i.e. not cunning.

barren i.e. of wit.

put down with an ordinary fool Compared with an unprofessional fool.

out of Off.

minister occasion Give him an opportunity (to make a joke) – as we say 'a peg to hang it on'.

take Consider.

these set kind i.e. professional kind.

zanies Professional imitators of Clowns, who created laughter by ludicrous imitation.

distempered Disordered. Therefore everything upsets him. These words of Olivia to Malvolio are well worth memorising.

bird-bolts Short, blunted arrows. The meaning of the phrase is that such a man makes light of things which displease him.

Mercury Messenger of the gods; also said to be the god of lying.

leasing Lying. The Clown graciously expresses his thanks to Olivia by saying that she has presented fools as better than they really are.

From the Count Orsino, is it? Olivia is quite used to his messengers!

well attended Refer to Orsino's directions in his last speech in the previous scene.

Now you see ... dislike it Notice that Olivia waits until Malvolio has gone out before saying this; she is considerate.

Jove King of the gods.

pia mater Brain; really the enveloping membrane of the brain.

What Who.

a plague ... herring Sir Toby has the hiccoughs.

sot Fool. Spoken to the Clown.

above heat More than thirst requires.

crowner Coroner – a crown official.

coz Contraction of 'cousin'. See note p.32.

sheriff's post Fixed outside a sheriff's house for the display of notices, proclamations, etc.

Why, of mankind A reply typical of the 'superior' Malvolio. Incidentally, note the dramatic irony.

squash Unripe pea-pod ('peascod').

codling Unripe apple.

in standing water At the turn of the tide.

well-favoured i.e. good-looking.

shrewishly Pertly.

Gentleman ... calls The very address indicates his superior tone.

which is she? Viola can tell quite well; she just wants to collect herself.

most radiant ... beauty A sample of Elizabethan affected court diction.

con Learn by heart.

comptible Sensitive.

sinister usage Discourtesy.

comedian Referring to Viola's 'part'.

I am not that I play Dramatic irony. (There are so many examples in this interview that they are not pointed out in the notes.)

you do usurp yourself In not giving yourself to Orsino.

from Away from.

forgive Excuse.

'tis not that time of moon with me I am not in the mood. The moon was supposed to influence the onset of madness. The Latin word for 'moon' is *luna*, whence 'lunatic'.

skipping Flippant.

swabber Sailor who washes down the decks. Viola repays Maria in her own coin. Having just come from a sea voyage she would be likely to have nautical terms 'fresh in memory'. But surely she forgets her part here: no gentleman would address a lady thus or make fun of her small stature.

hull Float.

some mollification for A sop for.

giant A sarcastic hit at Maria's stature.

Tell me your mind There is much to be said for attributing this speech to Olivia.

courtesy Ceremony.

your office What it is your duty to say.

alone concerns your ear Spoken, no doubt, with a 'catty' look at Maria, which Maria would return in full when she is forced to leave such an interesting meeting at the instance of Viola.

overture Declaration.

taxation Demand.

olive Symbol of peace.

as full of peace as matter i.e. there is nothing but peace in them.

entertainment Reception, as when we talk of 'entertaining' guests.

comfortable Comforting.

by the method In the same way.

this present Up to this moment.

in grain In a fast colour.

no copy i.e. by not marrying and leaving children.

schedules Lists.

labelled Attached, like a codicil.

indifferent See note p.34.

praise Appraise.

Could be but Would be but fittingly.

nonpareil Unequalled.

divulg'd Spoken of.

free Noble.

dimension Build, bodily form.

gracious Attractive.

flame i.e. heat, passion.

deadly life Deathlike life, 'living death' (oxymoron).

me For myself.

willow Symbol of grief.

cantons Songs, or perhaps cantos.

reverberate Echoing.

But Unless.

You might do much Emphasis on the 'you', as again four lines later.

parentage Olivia sees that Viola is of some breeding.

To tell me how he takes it A stratagem to see Viola again.

fee'd post Paid messenger.

his heart that The heart of the one whom. Dramatic irony – this is exactly what must happen when Olivia falls in love with Viola.

fivefold blazon Metaphor from a coat of arms. 'Fivefold' as five features are specified in the previous line.

soft A common exclamation of the time – as we should say, 'But, wait a moment . . . be careful.'

man Servant. If only Orsino were the servant and Viola the master making love to me. The sentence is unfinished to suggest Olivia's musing.

County's Count's.

he left this ring A lie to keep the servants' tongues from wagging. Note also the reason she gives that Viola should come again.

flatter with Give a false sense of security to.

Mine eye too great a flatterer for my mind That I have outstepped the bounds of my better judgment.

owe Possess, i.e. control.

Revision questions on Act I

1 In the first three scenes Shakespeare gives a wonderful impression of variety. How?

2 Give an account, with quotations, of the interview between Olivia and Viola.

3 During this interview does Viola ever forget that she is acting a part?

4 Give the story of the play and state the impression you have formed of the main characters up to the end of Act I.

Act II

Scene 1

Sebastian has been rescued by Antonio, a sea-captain, and a close friendship has sprung up between them.

This scene obviously should follow Act III, Sc.2, in which position it is usually acted.

Its importance to the plot is that the resemblance of Sebastian and Viola is emphasized, and, this having worked in their minds, the audience does not regard it beyond the bounds of probability, as might be the case if it were suddenly thrust at them. Sebastian decides to go to Orsino's court, which brings him into contact with the main action.

nor ... not In Elizabethan English a double negative intensifies the idea instead of logically cancelling it out.

malignancy Malevolence.

distemper See note p.36.

sooth Truly.

determinate On which I am determined.

extravagancy Vagrancy.

touch Trait.

charges me in manners Is incumbent on me as a matter of etiquette.

express myself Tell you who I am.

You must know, etc. Refer to the second paragraph of the introductory note to Act I, Sc.2, p.31.

Messaline An imaginary name.

breach Breaking, i.e. the breakers.

estimable wonder Wonder of estimation. cf. 'civil bounds', Act I, Sc.4.

overfar believe Go to such lengths as to believe.

entertainment See note p.37. 'Your entertainment' = 'my entertainment of you'. cf. 'your trouble' in Sebastian's reply. Antonio makes this apology now he knows Sebastian's parentage and position.

If you will not murder, etc. Perhaps an allusion to the superstition that a
man rescued from drowning will murder his rescuer, or perhaps he merely
means that he loves Sebastian so much that if he is not allowed to be his
servant it will be the death of him.
kindness Tenderness.
gentleness Good-will.

Scene 2

Viola realizes what we have heard from Olivia's lips – that Olivia
has fallen in love with her. Her resolution is characteristic of her – not
to cross the bridge till she comes to it.

Malvolio's churlishness is well illustrated here. Notice that Viola
does not give Olivia away to her steward. She sees 'how the land lies'
at once.

hardy Bold.
her eyes had lost The pre-occupation of her eyes had caused her to lose
control of.
pregnant Ready. The 'pregnant enemy' is the devil.
proper-false Handsome and yet false within.
set their forms Stamp their seals – continuing the metaphor in 'waxen'.
fadge Prosper.
monster i.e. because a beguiler.

Scene 3

Malvolio tries to put an end to the mirth of Sir Toby and his associates,
and this is the immediate cause of the conspiracy against him round
which the sub-plot revolves. The time of the scene is settled by Maria's
'since the youth of the count's was *to-day* with my lady'.

diluculo surgere The full proverb is 'Diluculo surgere saluberrimum est',
'Early to rise is most healthful'.
stoup Flagon.
'We three.' An inn-sign representing two heads, with the caption 'We three
loggerheads [fools] be', the spectator, of course, making the third.
catch Round.
breast Voice.
Pigrogromitus, etc. See note on 'Quinapalus', p.35.
leman Sweetheart.

impeticos thy gratillity Put your gratuity in my petticoat (intentional nonsense).

whipstock Handle of a whip, i.e. Malvolio's nose is sharp at smelling out faults (as we are soon to see).

Myrmidons Strictly speaking, followers of Achilles, here used for officers of the law, meaning that the haunts of law officers are not bottle-ale houses.

testril of Sixpence from. Sir Andrew does just what Sir Toby does (and says what he says).

good Virtuous. The Clown may have meant a life of excitement and fun and Sir Andrew misunderstood him.

O mistress mine This song appears in Morley's *Consort* [concert] *Lessons* (1599).

sweeting A term of endearment.

plenty Profit.

and twenty And twenty times sweet, or perhaps referring to the maiden's age.

contagious Sir Toby tries to lead Sir Andrew on to use long, inappropriate words.

welkin dance Sky turn round.

draw ... weaver Transport even a psalm-singing weaver. Weavers were reputed to be given to singing psalms. Many were Calvinist refugees from the Netherlands.

dog An old hand.

By'r lady By our lady, i.e. the Virgin Mary.

some dogs ... well Perhaps said holding his hands out for another 'testril'.

Cataian Native of Cataia, or Cathay, i.e. China, a term of reproach.

politicians Schemers.

Peg-a-Ramsey The title of an old song.

Tilly-vally An expression of contempt.

Beshrew me An imprecation.

honesty Sense of propriety.

tinkers Proverbially given to drink and bad language.

coziers' Cobblers'.

Sneck up! Equivalent to 'Be hanged to you!'

round Plain.

harbours you Gives you shelter, a roof over your head.

disorders Misdemeanours.

an See note, p.33.

Is't even so? Expressive of disgust at their general behaviour and intoxicated state.

Dost thou think ... ale? This remark 'hits off' Malvolio's character exactly.

by Saint Anne An oath to provoke Malvolio further. As a Puritan, Malvolio would be opposed to swearing at all, let alone the invocation of a Catholic saint (mother of the Virgin Mary).

ginger i.e. as a spice in ale.

rub ... crumbs i.e. to clean it. His steward's chain of office is meant.

rule Conduct.

shake your ears Implying that he is a donkey.

the field i.e. to a duel.

gull Fool.

nayword Byword.

recreation Laughing-stock.

possess Tell.

puritan Some editors think Shakespeare is expressing his own contempt for Puritans here.

exquisite Subtle.

time-pleaser Time-server.

affectioned Affected.

cons state without book Learns by heart impressive phrases to repeat without the book.

swarths Swaths, 'by the ream'.

the best persuaded With the best opinion.

his grounds of faith The foundation of his faith.

expressure Expression.

feelingly personated Exactly described.

forgotten i.e. written a long time ago.

Ass, I doubt not On the surface agreement with Sir Andrew, but also a hidden address to him.

physic Medicine.

construction How he puts it together.

event Issue, result.

Penthesilea Queen of the Amazons. Kindly sarcasm at little Maria.

Before me Equivalent to 'My goodness!'

beagle A small breed of dog.

recover Gain.

out Out of pocket, or perhaps simply mistaken.

cut Fool. Literally, a horse with a docked tail employed on farm work.

burn some sack Warm some wine.

Scene 4

The qualities of the Duke apparent in the two previous scenes in which he appears are re-emphasized. His opinions are as changeable as his

likes and dislikes. Contrast 11. 17–20, 33–6, and the speech beginning
'There is no woman's sides'. There is now no doubt of Viola's love
for Orsino, hinted at at the end of Act I, Sc.4.

Notice the dramatic irony consequent upon Viola's disguise, particularly at the end of the scene.

morrow Morning.

but Just.

antique Quaint.

recollected terms Set or borrowed words.

Feste This shows where the Fool went to when he took French leave from
Olivia's house. See Act I, Sc.5. — Orsino's Palace

motions Emotions.

favour i.e. face.

your favour A slight emphasis on the 'your' would make the double
meaning obvious to any audience.

complexion Appearance.

wears to Metaphor from the 'sit' of a garment.

sways level Metaphor from a balance; i.e. there are no fits and starts in
their affection.

worn Worn out.

bent Metaphor from a bow taking the strain.

spinsters Spinners, the literal sense.

bones Bobbins.

Do use to Are accustomed to.

silly sooth Simple truth.

old Implying a better.

away i.e. to me.

cypress A coffin of cypress wood. The cypress (like the yew) was a symbol
of mourning.

part Perhaps a metaphor from acting.

so true i.e. as I.

Give me ... leave thee A polite dismissal.

melancholy god Saturn.

changeable taffeta Shot silk.

opal A jewel which changes colour in different lights as shot silk does.

their intent every where The place they make for constantly changing.

it i.e. going to sea.

nothing No settled intention.

cruelty Viola's last word to Olivia in her previous interview.

world Material things.

parts Possessions.

pranks Adorns.

cloyment Surfeit.

revolt Nausea.

as hungry as the sea The Duke is fond of toying with this simile.
  cf. I,1,11.

compare Here a noun.

Our shows are more than will Our protestations are more than our
  will-power to make them effective. The next sentence amplifies the
  meaning.

yet I know not She is thinking of the 'chance' of Act I, Sc.2.

give no place Give place to nothing.

denay Denial.

Scene 5

Malvolio, ripe to be duped, falls an easy prey to Maria's trap. Much
of the fun is derived from the asides of the onlookers and their eagerness
to see and yet not be seen. It is a matter for wonder that Maria is
not one of them.

scruple Scrap.

sheep-biter Sheep-stealer.

bear-baiting A popular Elizabethan sport.

metal of India i.e. gold; 'girl of gold'.

Close Get well hidden.

she Olivia.

Maria once told me ... me Maria has well prepared the ground.

affect Have affection for.

I have heard herself ... complexion Imagination, or has his mind,
  'growing by what it feeds on', exaggerated beyond recognition some
  compliment from Olivia?

over-weening Conceited.

jets Struts.

advanced Raised.

'Slight A contraction of 'God's light' – an ingenious way of getting round a
  law which forbade the profane use of the name of God on the stage.

Strachy Probably an allusion to a character of a play or story fashionable
  at the time. This kind of allusion presents difficulties for us, but would have
  been understood by Shakespeare's audiences.

yeoman of the wardrobe An actual office in Elizabethan times.

Jezebel Sir Andrew knows merely that it is uncomplimentary.

blows him Puffs him out.

state Chair of state.

stone-bow Cross-bow for flinging stones.

branched With designs of branches, leaves, etc.

day-bed Sofa.

humour of state Air of one in authority.

travel of regard Look round.

my – some He was going to say 'my chain', forgetting he would no longer be a steward. It is by such small touches that Shakespeare is so true to life.

cars Chariots.

control Authority.

woodcock Supposed to be a bird of low intelligence (like the gull, see note p.42.

gin Trap.

spirit of humours The guardian spirit of men's moods.

in contempt of question Without doubt.

Why that? Sir Andrew is too dull to see that Malvolio is referring to the letter.

soft See note p.38.

Lucrece The head of the Roman matron Lucretia was a favourite figure for ladies' seals.

numbers Metre.

brock Badger. A term of contempt.

Lucrece knife Lucretia stabbed herself.

fustian Bombastic.

What dish What a dish.

the staniel checks at it The hawk turns from its proper prey in order to follow it. In Shakespeare's time metaphors from hawking and hunting would be as familiar as metaphors from cricket today.

formal capacity Average intelligence.

Sowter … fox This particular dog (Sowter is a dog's name) will cry when it picks up the 'cold scent', though to any ordinary dog it would be as strongly false as the scent of a fox.

faults A 'fault' is the hunting term for when the scent fails.

consonancy Agreement.

probation Examination.

O shall end The idea is similar to that in Sir Toby's next speech.

simulation Disguise.

revolve Turn things over in your mind.

blood Courage.

slough Metaphor from a snake casting its skin.

opposite Perverse.

a kinsman Obviously Sir Toby is implied.

tang Twang. An onomatopoeic word.

singularity Being 'different'.

yellow stockings ... cross-gartered Very fashionable at the time, but, it appears, hated by Olivia, as Maria well knew when she tricked Malvolio into wearing them (see end of scene). Incidentally yellow stockings were not likely to be worn by a *conscientious* Puritan.

In some representations of *Twelfth Night* Viola as a page is dressed in yellow stockings, the inference being that although 'Cesario' is wearing a colour Olivia abhors, her love is so great that beside it a personal whim is of no account.

I say, remember Perhaps emphasized because there was nothing to remember. No doubt Maria counted on his conceit supplying the self-deception.

alter services Change places.

champain Open country.

discovers Reveals. Singular because the two subjects are associated. There are many similar instances. It was quite a common Elizabethan usage, and conversely we find a plural verb with a subject-word in the singular but whose idea is plural.

point-devise To the letter.

baffle By being 'opposite' with him.

jade Fool.

strange, stout Reserved, proud.

even ... on As quickly as I can get them on.

Sophy Shah of Persia.

gull-catcher See note on 'woodcock' above.

thy foot o' my neck As a sign of complete subjection, as a 'bond-slave'.

play my freedom at tray-trip Play at tray-trip (a dice game) with my freedom as the stake.

the image of it leaves him i.e. he is brought down to earth.

aqua-vitae Brandy.

unsuitable to her disposition As she is mourning for her brother.

Tartar Tartarus, the classical hell.

one One of the party.

Revision questions on Act II

1 What fresh light is thrown on the character of Viola in Sc.2 and in Sc.4.

2 'I am for all waters' (IV,2). Illustrate the Clown's ready adaptation of himself to his company (from Scenes 3 and 4).

3 Imagine you are producing *Twelfth Night* and write Malvolio's part in Sc.5 with extended stage directions for the actor.

4 Give a brief account of Malvolio's discovery of the letter and say what impressions you form of his character from this scene.

Act III

Scene 1

Viola carries out Orsino's command given at the end of Act II, Sc.4. She meets with mixed company. Olivia 'lets herself go' and openly avows her love for Viola. Her bearing in this speech is in marked contrast to the polite and proper demeanour of each so far. The rhyme emphasizes it. The scene closes with a definite invitation to Viola to come again.

Save thee God save thee.

tabor Small drum. Part of the stock-in-trade of professional fools.

by Such 'dallying nicely' with words was very popular in Elizabethan times and therefore frequently occurred on the stage.

churchman Clergyman.

lies Lives.

To see this age! 'What is the world coming to!'

cheveril Kid.

the wrong side ... outward i.e. a wrong meaning understood.

dally nicely with words Split hairs with meanings of words, 'corrupt' words (as the Clown says later).

bonds Really '*broken* bonds'.

late See note p.32.

at the Count Orsino's See Act II, Sc.4.

orb Earth.

but Except.

pass upon me A fencing metaphor. Equivalent to 'get one across me'. Used literally by Sir Toby in Sc.4.

expenses Euphemism for a 'tip'.

commodity Consignment.

sick for one i.e Orsino's. In the acting the double meaning would be quite clear from the emphasis on the 'my' which follows.

there Referring to the coin Viola has given him.

use Usury, interest.

Lord Pandarus of Phrygia Helped Troilus and Cressida to meet. Phrygia was a kingdom of Asia Minor.

Cressida. Troilus Cressida vowed eternal love to Troilus, but turned out to be faithless.

a beggar For a beggar. It was after her desertion of Troilus that Cressida became a beggar.

construe Explain. He uses a high-sounding word in mock-heroic style.

craves The meaning here is 'requires', 'necessitates' (not 'desires').

haggard Wild and untrained hawk, which would 'check' (see note p.45) at *every* bird.

Dieu vous garde, monsieur God save you, sir.

Et vous aussi; votre serviteur And you also; (I am) your servant.

I hope, sir Sir Andrew soon stops talking French when he discovers that Viola knows the language. He had merely got a few phrases 'ready' to impress her.

encounter Go towards. Satire of the affected courtier's style was common on the Elizabethan stage.

trade Business.

list Goal.

Taste Try.

understand The first time this word is used there is a pun on the literal meaning 'stand under'.

prevented Anticipated.

pregnant See note p.40

vouchsafed Vouchsafing attention.

I'll get ... ready See note on 'I hope, sir', above.

lowly feigning Being 'humble' in the Uriah Heep sense.

by your leave An apology for interrupting her. cf. 'give me leave', below.

another suit i.e. your own.

music from the spheres As the spheres revolved round the earth they were supposed to give forth music, but it was too beautiful to be heard by human ears.

did Caused.

abuse Deceive.

hard Unfavourable. For 'construction' see note p.42.

sit Remain.

stake See note on 'bear-baiting', p.44.

receiving Quickness 'in the up-take'.

cypress Crape.

degree. grize Both words mean step.

a vulgar proof Commonly proved. 'Vulgar' = 'common' meaning 'general', without implying contempt as in 'Common room', *Book of Common Prayer*.

proper Fine. cf. note p.43.

westward-ho! A cry Shakespeare and his audience would many times have heard on the Thames quays.

attend Wait on.

That you do think ... are i.e. that you forget your rank (and possibly self-respect). Olivia's reply is that she forgets her rank and Viola's in speaking as she has done.

fool Dupe.

would Wishes to.

maidhood Maidenhood, virginity.

maugre In spite of (from Fr. *malgré*).

wit Good sense.

Do not extort ... this clause Do not force justification for yourself from what I have just said.

For that Because.

cause Cause to woo.

reason thus with reason fetter Bind reason with reason as follows.

for thou perhaps ... love Surely Olivia does not expect Viola to fail to see through this pretence!

Scene 2

Sir Andrew is stung with jealousy of his rival Viola and, for a bit of fun, Sir Toby rouses him to take revenge in a duel.

I saw ... me In the previous scene.

orchard Garden.

argument Proof.

Noah ... sailor Referring, of course, to the account of the flood in *Genesis*.

She did show favour etc. Fabian very ingeniously twists the situation and 'extorts reasons' to make Sir Andrew stay.

fire-new ... mint i.e. not yet in circulation, *brand* new.

balked Missed, shirked.

sailed into the north cf. the expression 'giving anyone *cold* looks'.

policy Diplomacy, in the rather bad sense of 'scheming'. 'Politician' has the same disparaging sense.

lief Soon.

Brownist Member of a Puritan sect founded by Robert Browne.

eleven Why 'eleven'?

curst Sharp (i.e. in the tone of the letter).

how About being.

'thou 'st.' It was an insult so to address anyone who was a social equal and with whom one was not on terms of familiarity. 'Thou' was the address from masters to servants or between close companions.

bed of Ware Capable of holding twelve people, belonging to the inn at Ware, in Hertfordshire.

gall Bitterness.

cubiculo Cubicle, little room.

dear In the sense of 'expensive'.

wainropes Wagon-ropes.

Opposite Opponent.

youngest wren of nine And therefore the smallest.

the spleen A fit of laughter.

renegado Renegade.

passages of grossness Acts of stupidity.

pedant Schoolmaster. To keep a school in a Church was by no means unusual in Elizabethan times.

the new map Obviously a map well-known to an average audience at that time. Shakespeare's plays are full of topical references like this. The point of some is quite lost, but there are others, like this one, whose effect we can catch if we read the plays with imagination and consider the effect on us of a reference on the stage today to a topic which is in everybody's mouth.

Scene 3

This scene is usually preceded, in stage presentations, by Act II, Scene 1 (see p.39).

Sebastian arrives on the scene of the action, thereby presaging a greater tangle of mistaken identity but also an ultimate solution. Antonio gives him his purse and tells him to make free with it, arranging to meet him later.

From here to the end of the play all happens on the same day – in Act V Antonio tells the Duke that Sebastian only came to the town 'to-day'. Between the end of this scene and the end of the next is less than half an hour, as Antonio also says that between his giving Sebastian his purse and his arrest was 'not half an hour'.

jealousy Apprehension.

skilless Inexperienced; the word brings home the different conditions of travel in those days.

uncurrent pay Coin which is not legal tender, and therefore valueless. Metaphorically referring to mere thanks, which are meaningless without the will to *do* something.

worth Wealth.

What's to do? What shall we do?

reliques Monuments (not ruins), 'memorials' and 'things of fame'.

renown Make renowned.

I do not without danger ... streets See Antonio's soliloquy at the end of Act II, Sc.1.

count his A wrong construction, due to the erroneous belief that the 's was a contraction of 'his', whereas really it signifies Count's.

answer'd Atoned for.

bloody argument Cause of bloodshed.

traffic Trade.

lapsed Caught lapsing.

toy Trifle, knick-knack.

store Possessions.

idle markets Purchases of luxuries.

Scene 4

Just at a time when Olivia sends for Malvolio because 'he is sad and civil', he appears smiling, in 'yellow stockings and cross-gartered'. As he is coming Maria suggests to Olivia that he must be mad. Olivia has not long to consider the spectacle, however, for very soon Viola is announced. After bantering Malvolio, the conspirators determine to use the pretext of his madness to have him bound and locked up in a dark room.

On Viola's return from Olivia, Sir Toby and Fabian manage to bring about a duel between Viola and Sir Andrew, both persuaded their opponent is 'a very devil', and scared out of their wits. Viola is prevented from going back to the house to seek safe-conduct of Olivia and fights rather than reveal her identity, yet 'A little thing would tell them how much I lack of a man'. Just as the fight is about to start, in rushes Antonio in Viola's defence, taking her for Sebastian. Antonio is recognized by Officers, and in his predicament asks Viola for his purse (given to Sebastian). Viola, of course, knows nothing about it, but offers him half her 'having' in recognition of his timely help and sympathy for his present trouble. With bitter words about ingratitude, Antonio is dragged off. Before he goes, he addresses Viola as 'Sebastian', however, and light begins to dawn on her.

him Viola.

he says Suppose he says.

of On.

For youth ... borrow'd If she only knew it, a poor commentary on the character of Viola.

sad Serious.

possessed i.e. with a devil. Maria again prepares the ground well. Would it have occurred to Olivia that Malvolio was mad had Maria not put it into her head? Similarly, after Malvolio's appearance, she eggs him on by 'Why appear you with this ridiculous boldness before my lady?' and later, 'My lady would not lose him for more than I'll say.'

daws Jackdaws.

midsummer madness At midsummer people were supposed to be more inclined to madness. cf. *A Midsummer Night's Dream*.

entreat him back See the first line of the scene.

Let ... special care of him There is no doubt that Malvolio was an efficient steward.

miscarry Come to mischance.

consequently Subsequently.

habit Manner.

limed Caught (as a bird with bird-lime).

degree Rank, position.

incredulous Incredible.

unsafe Unsure.

in little In small compass.

Legion A personification of 'all the devils of hell'. See Mark, 5,9, Luke, 8,30.

man Fabian adopts a free and easy manner in order to have the pleasure of seeing Malvolio rise up against it.

private Privacy.

hollow Referring to Malvolio's affectation of dignity in his speech.

bawcock Fine fellow (Fr. 'beau coq').

cherry-pit A game in which cherry-stones were pitched into a hole ('pit').

collier Applied to the devil because of his blackness.

If this were played ... fiction A clever stroke giving the illusion of reality.

genius Spirit.

take air and taint Metaphor of something going bad through exposure to the air.

The house ... quieter i.e. when he has been put away.

dark room and bound The old treatment of lunatics (enough to drive a sane person mad).

carry Carry on with.

bring ... bar A legal metaphor.

May i.e. festive.

admire The same as 'wonder'.

note Comment.

in my sight See Sc.2.

– less Said under his breath. Notice the position of Fabian's next interjection, and its significance for everyone except Sir Andrew.

windy i.e. safe.

but my hope is better Notice the difference between what Sir Andrew means and what he says.

occasion Opportunity.

commerce Business.

bum-baily Bailiff.

draw i.e. thy sword.

approbation Credit.

gives him out Reveals. Olivia could not help but notice Viola's good breeding. See her speech immediately after Viola's departure at the end of Act I, Sc.5.

clodpole Blockhead.

cockatrices Fabulous creatures.

give ... leave So that Olivia knows nothing about it.

presently At once – the literal meaning of the word.

laid Staked.

unchary Carelessly, heedlessly.

jewel ... picture A be-jewelled miniature.

it hath no tongue to vex you Implying a contrast with herself.

that I'll deny 'That' here is a relative pronoun.

That honour ... give That may be given upon the asking consistent with honour.

thee Notice the use of 'thee' in this farewell. Throughout the conversation until now Olivia has used 'you'. Sir Toby addresses Viola by the familiar 'thee', but Viola does not lose sight of her position and answers him with 'you'.

attends Waits for.

dismount thy tuck Draw thy sword. Sir Toby uses court style to the page boy.

yare Quick.

dubbed ... consideration Dubbed knight with unhacked rapier for civil service in peace (and not war service in battle).

hob, nob Same as 'give't or take't'.

conduct Escort, safe-conduct.

Signior Fabian ... return In order to see that Viola does not run back to the house.

mortal arbitrement Fight to the death.

read him by his form Judge him by his appearance. It was necessary to tell Viola that Sir Andrew was not such a fool as he looked or she would not have been so frightened.

sir priest 'Sir' was a title commonly given to clergymen in those days.

firago Really a brawling *woman*, but Sir Andrew is no scholar. Besides, is not the application to Viola dramatic irony?

stuck Thrust.

answer Return stroke.

Sophy See note p.46.

motion Proposition.

I'll ride your horse Instead of giving it to Viola, he will keep it for himself.

ride you i.e. manage you.

take up Make up. The phrase has the opposite meaning from what it would have today.

is as horribly conceited Has the same horrible notion.

supportance Upholding.

duello Rules of duelling.

have done ... defy you Antonio takes 'his' side whether 'he' is in the right or wrong.

undertaker Meddler, one who undertakes things which are not his concern.

anon i.e. when the officers have gone.

for that I promised you i.e. his horse.

having Property.

my present The money I have upon me.

my deserts ... persuasion I need to persuade you of my kindnesses.

upbraid you with Throw back at you.

venerable worth Worthy of veneration.

feature Appearance.

unkind Unnatural.

beauteous-evil Those who look beautiful but are really evil. In this speech Antonio expresses the very same thought that Viola had expressed to the Captain in Act I, Sc.2.

trunks, o'erflourish'd Chests carved on top.

couplet Couple.

glass Mirror. When she looks in the mirror she appears just the same as Sebastian. Refer to the third speech of Sebastian in Act II, Sc.1.

Still Always.

salt. fresh Notice the antithesis.

'Slid See note on ''Slight', p.44.

never draw thy sword The Officers are still about.

Revision questions on Act III

1 'If this were played upon a stage now, I could condemn it as an improbable fiction.' Do you agree?

2 What is your opinion of Viola's conduct in the predicaments in which she finds herself in Sc.4?

3 Show how plot and sub-plot are bound together in this Act.

4 What confusions arise in Act III owing to disguise and resemblance?

Act IV

Scene 1

The Clown, Sir Toby, Sir Andrew and Fabian all take Sebastian for Viola. Sir Andrew, who has run after Viola to set on 'him', thinking 'him' a coward, comes up with Sebastian, cuffs him and, in return, gets more than he has bargained for. Sir Toby thereupon starts to fight Sebastian, when Olivia suddenly appears and, infuriated to see him attacking 'Cesario', curtly dismisses him, makes an apology to Sebastian and asks him in. Sebastian is nonplussed, but nevertheless accepts the invitation.

sent for you Of course, it is for 'Cesario' the Clown has been sent.

Go to An expression of mild reproof. Curiously enough, we say, 'Come, come'.

clear Rid.

held out Sustained, kept up, i.e. the pretence not to know him.

the world, will prove a cockney (At this rate) every one in the world will become affected.

Greek Jester.

open Generous. Sebastian is 'open' with Antonio's money!

fourteen years' purchase A legal term in the purchase of land. The usual price in the time of Shakespeare was twelve years' purchase, therefore fourteen would be a good price (i.e. fourteen times the annual rent).

have I met you again? Refer to the end of Act III, Sc.4.

This will I tell See p.29.

action of battery Summons for assault.

well fleshed i.e. having 'tasted blood'.

malapert Saucy.

Hold, Toby Olivia has heard of what is going on from the Clown and has come at once.

Rudesby Rude fellow, ruffian.

extent i.e. assault.

fruitless Pointless.

botch'd See note p.39. There were still more 'pranks' of which Olivia knew nothing – as yet!

thou ... go Naturally Sebastian shows reluctance.

deny Refuse.

Beshrew Curse.

What relish is in this? What can I make of this?

Or ... or Either ... or.

Lethe In Greek mythology, the river of forgetfulness.

Scene 2

Malvolio, now locked up in a dark room, is teased by the Clown, talking to him as Sir Topas the curate and then in his own voice. Sir Toby thinks the joke has gone far enough, as Olivia is now so annoyed with him, and asks the Clown to bring things to a safe conclusion, if possible. The Clown therefore accedes to Malvolio's request to take a letter to Olivia. Notice how differently Malvolio addresses the Clown when he wants to get something out of him.

Maria disappears from the play.

Sir Topas See note on 'sir priest', p.53.

dissemble Disguise.

to be said ... as fairly It is as well to be reputed an honest man and a good host.

careful Full of care – the literal meaning.

competitors Confederates.

Bonos dies Another inaccurate 'Spanish' phrase 'good-day' (*Buenos dias*). (See note on *Castiliano vulgo* p.33).

hermit of Prague No doubt another imaginary character of the Clown's invention.

King Gorboduc An old British king, known to an Elizabethan audience through a play *Gorboduc*.

modest Moderate.

bay-windows Windows where the recess of the windows came *into* the room, and not outwards as in modern bay-windows.

barricadoes Ramparts.

clear-stories Clerestories (the derivation is obvious).

obstruction i.e. of light.

the Egyptians in their fog See Exodus, 10,21–3.

abused See note p.48, though here the word has a stronger sense and might be rendered 'maltreated'.

constant question Consistent questioning.

Pythagoras Greek philosopher who believed in the transmigration of souls.

allow of thy wits Admit you are in your right mind.

woodcock See note p.45.

for all waters Able to put my hand to anything, take any part.

delivered Set free.

so far in offence Refer to the previous scene.

'Hey, Robin,' From an ancient Scottish ballad, later printed in Percy's *Reliques of Ancient English Poetry* (1765).

perdy Corruption of Fr. 'par dieu' = 'by God'.

besides Out of.

propertied Used me as their property.

Advise you Be careful. The dashes show the change from the Clown speaking in his own voice to that of 'Sir Topas'.

endeavour thyself Try.

bibble-babble Idle, foolish talk. cf. 'tittle-tattle'.

shent Reproved.

Well-a-day An exclamation of grief.

advantage thee more Be of more advantage to you. (Malvolio is no doubt aware of the Clown's partiality for 'tips'.)

Vice The Vice was a conventional character of the Morality plays (in which the characters were various qualities, e.g. Pride, Ambition), the precursors of Elizabethan drama. He invariably raised a laugh by belabouring the Devil with a wooden dagger and trying to cut his (long) nails.

goodman Not to be taken literally; just a cheery form of address.

Scene 3

Sebastian is lost in wonder at the turn events are taking. Olivia comes in with the Priest all ready and persuades Sebastian to promise to marry her at once.

pearl This turns out to be an engagement ring.

Elephant See III,3,39.

was i.e. had booked a room.

credit Message.

discourse Reason.

trust Conviction. Antithetical to 'distrust'.

take ... dispatch Get a grip of affairs and make speedy arrangements to deal with them. 'Affairs' is the object of 'take', and 'dispatch' of 'give'.

deceivable deceptive.

chantry Chapel, i.e. the private chapel of Olivia's house. It was usual for the stately homes of Shakespeare's time to have their own chapel, and some in Warwickshire, Shakespeare's own county, to go no farther, may still be seen.

Whiles Until. 'While' is still used with this meaning in the West Riding of Yorkshire.

to note To be made known.

What i.e. at which.

fairly note Approve.

Revision questions on Act IV

1 What confusion does Sebastian cause when he appears on the scene of the action?

2 Describe the part played by the Clown in Sc.2.

3 What is shown of Malvolio's character by (a) his answers to 'Sir Topas', (b) his pleading with the Clown?

4 Is Sebastian's action understandable in taking Olivia to wife at such short notice?

Act V

The Duke comes to make love to Olivia in person. There are various misunderstandings and charges against Viola, due to her resemblance to Sebastian, from which she fails convincingly to extricate herself. Then 'confusion worse confounded' is all at once made clear on the appearance of Sebastian. The Duke takes Viola as his wife, and Sebastian takes Olivia.

Malvolio is released. We hear that Sir Toby has married Maria out of admiration for her skill in framing the plot against him. Everyone is happy except Malvolio, whose final words are the only jarring note. But we soon forget this in a jolly song from the Clown.

his letter i.e. Malvolio's. See Act IV, Sc.2.

trappings Hangers-on.

I know thee well See Act II, Sc.4.

as kisses It takes four people to make two kisses.

grace Virtue – with a pun on his title or his 'graciousness'. (cf. the pun on 'double-dealing'.)

Primo, secundo, tertio First, second, third.

play i.e. at dice.

triplex Triple time in music; probably the Clown means music for dancing.

Saint Bennet A well-known London church. 'Bennet' is a contraction of 'Benedict'.

throw Metaphor from dice-playing.

Vulcan Roman god of fire and forging.

bawbling Insignificant. The vessel was a 'bauble'.

unprizable Valueless.

scatheful Harmful.

bottom Vessel.

fraught Cargo. cf. *freight*.

from Candy On the way from Candia (Crete).

When your young nephew Titus A touch of circumstantial detail.

in the streets Actually, according to Rowe's stage direction, Act III, Sc.4 happens 'in Olivia's garden', but it is quite evident that at the end of the scene Shakespeare has a street scene in mind. In an Elizabethan representation, where the stage would look exactly the same for either, it would matter little (even if it were noticed).

brabble Brawl, quarrel. An onomatopoeic word.

distraction Madness.

dear Earnest.

ground We use the plural, 'grounds'.

pure Purely.

into Unto.

face me out cf. Malvolio's expression in Act IV, Sc.2, 'face me out of my wits'.

three months Not consistent with Valentine's first speech in Act I, Sc.4, but Shakespeare was never very careful over details. The life and spirit of a play were what mattered to him.

Cesario ... me Sebastian has been delayed, as Sir Toby has found an opportunity to measure swords with him.

fat The same meaning as 'fulsome'.

ingrate and unauspicious Now *un*grateful and *in*auspicious.

Even ... him A polite way of saying, 'Do what you like – I don't care'.

the Egyptian thief Thyamis, a robber chief, who, overcome by another band of robbers, tried to slay a captured maiden with whom he had fallen in love, rather than let her fall into the hands of his enemies.

non-regardance Disregard.

minion i.e. favourite.

tender Regard.

apt Readily.

strangle thy propriety Deny your true identity.

in my function By me in my official position.

sow'd a grizzle on thy case Scattered a grizzly beard on your skin.

thine own ... overthrow You will be tripped up by your own craftiness.

little i.e. just a little.

coxcomb A humorous word for the head.

I had rather than forty pound cf. Sir Andrew's expression in Act II, Sc.3, 'I had rather than forty shillings'. Forty is a common Biblical number, and many English expressions have their origin in the Bible.

incardinate Sir Andrew's rendering of 'incarnate'.

othergates Otherwise.

passy measures pavin 'Slow-coach'. Metaphor from a slow and grave dance measure.

be dressed i.e. have our wounds dressed.

an ass-head ... gull In his drunken condition Sir Toby has not the same control over his words and unguardedly tells Sir Andrew what he really thinks of him.

wit and safety A due regard for my safety.

regard Look. The 'strange regard', of course, was not owing to Olivia's annoyance at his attack on Sir Toby, but to his being Viola's 'double'.

perspective i.e. glass or arrangment of mirrors which makes an optical illusion.

Do I stand there? Viola must be standing out of the way on Sebastian's entrance, for he does not see her until now.

deity Divine power.

Of charity Out of kindness.

Of Messaline See Sebastian's second speech in Act II, Sc.1.

Such a Sebastian Such a Sebastian as you.

suited Dressed.

dimension See note p.38.

goes even Coincides, fits in.

record Remembrance.

lets Prevents, hinders.

cohere. jump Both have the meaning of 'the same', 'equal'.

Where At whose house.

weeds Clothes.

occurrence of my fortune My business.

bias Here a woman's leaning towards a woman is meant.

right noble is his blood We can assume that Orsino had at least heard of Sebastian's father. Sebastian's father knew Orsino, for Viola said she had heard her father name Orsino (I,2), and Orsino must have heard of Sebastian's father, for Sebastian took it as a matter of course that anyone so well-known as his father would be known to Antonio (II,1).

glass Referring to his 'perspective' metaphor.

over-swear Swear over again.

that orbed continent the fire The sun keep the fire.

action i.e. A lawsuit.

durance Prison.

enlarge i.e. set free.

distract See note on 'distraction', p.59.

extracting frenzy Absorbing madness, a madness drawing all other thoughts away. Olivia would stress the first syllable, to bring out the contrast with '*dis*tract'.

clearly Entirely.

holds at the stave's end i.e. keeps off.

skills Matters.

delivers Repeats the words of.

art thou mad? The Clown evidently starts to read the letter in humorous imitation of a raving madman.

vox A loud voice.

to read his right wits is to read thus Because he is a madman.

perpend Consider. An extravagant word humorously used.

Read it you Olivia is not in the mood for fooling.

cousin See note p.32.

savours cf. the Duke's expression earlier in the scene, 'savours nobly'.

deliver'd Set free. (See note on 'enlarge' above.)

proper Own.

from See note p.37.

hand. phrase. seal These were the things he first noticed when he found the letter (II,5).

lights Marks.

geck Dupe.

character Hand-writing.

presuppos'd Suggested beforehand.

practice Plot.

shrewdly Cruelly.

Upon Owing to, on account of.

uncourteous parts Discourteous qualities.

we had conceiv'd against him At which we had been indignant.

importance Importunity.

he hath married her When has he had opportunity? (At the moment he has gone half-drunk to bed to have his wounds dressed.) Another example of Shakespeare's scant attention to detail.

pluck on Excite.

poor fool Said kindly. 'Fool' could be a term of pity in Elizabethan English. In *As You Like It*, for instance, it is applied to a wounded stag.

baffled Treated contemptuously.

thrown This variation, instead of 'thrust', the word Malvolio actually used, is one of those little touches by which Shakespeare gives a sense of reality. We do not remember things word for word.

interlude Little comedy.

golden Metaphor for that which is best and highest.

convents Is convenient.

habits Dress.

SONG It was customary to end a comedy with a jolly song from the Clown.

and a little tiny boy The redundant 'and' is frequent in popular ballads. The following line is a common refrain.

toy See note p.51. When he was a boy people thought nothing of his foolish acts. But he goes on to say that he could not get on as a knave and a thief in manhood.

had I had.

And we'll strive ... day Corresponding to the modern 'Coming shortly'.

Revision questions on Act V

1 Comment on Antonio's conduct as a prisoner before Orsino.

2 When had Sir Toby and Maria a chance to get married? Does it seem natural to you that Maria would *want* to marry Sir Toby?

3 Write a brief account of the last Act, showing how all the loose ends of the plot are brought together and neatly tied.

4 Are you satisfied with the ending of *Twelfth Night*? Consider especially the 'pairing off' and the figure cut by Malvolio.

General Questions

1 Make a list in order of the disposition of scenes as between main and sub-plot. Then indicate the changes from verse to prose or prose to verse in the scenes, stating what you think is the reason for each change.

2 Which character do you think is the chief connecting link between plot and sub-plot? By close reference to the play explain in what way.

3 Point out all the examples of mistaken identity in the play, excluding Viola as Cesario.

4 How far is *Twelfth Night* a comedy of deception, and how far a comedy of *self*-deception?

5 State and illustrate the varied means used by Shakespeare to provide comedy in *Twelfth Night*.

6 '*Twelfth Night* takes place nominally in Illyria, but we are really never very far from London.' Discuss this statement.

7 Discuss and illustrate from incidents and conversation Viola's (*a*) common sense, (*b*) sense of honour.

8 Compare and contrast (*a*) the characters of Viola and Olivia as young women in love or, (*b*) the characters of Maria and Malvolio as servants to Olivia.

9 Show what you learn of Olivia's character from her relations with Orsino, Sir Toby, Malvolio and the Clown.

10 'Thy mind is very opal.' Do you consider this a true criticism of Orsino?

11 What qualities of Malvolio are held up to ridicule in the play? Refer to his own words and actions and the opinions of other characters in the play to illustrate your remarks.

12 How far did Malvolio deserve his discomfiture?

13 Show from the play what opinions of Malvolio are held by (*a*) himself, (*b*) Olivia, (*c*) Maria.

14 Malvolio and Sir Andrew are both fools. What is the difference between them?

15 What is it about Sir Toby that makes him Sir Andrew's 'hero'?

16 'We ought not to like this drunken reveller, but we all do' (p.26). Do you agree with this estimate?

17 Hazlitt says of *Twelfth Night*, 'It makes us laugh at the follies of mankind, not despise them'. How far does this criticism reflect your attitude to (*a*) Malvolio, (*b*) Sir Toby, (*c*) Sir Andrew?

18 Does Feste come up to Viola's idea of a Fool, that 'he must observe their mood on whom he jests, the quality of persons, and the time'? Illustrate your answer by careful reference to the play.

19 What part is taken in the play by Fabian?

20 Refer to two songs in *Twelfth Night* and show their suitability to the circumstances in which they are sung.

21 Take three occasions where rhyming verse is used and state the reason for it in each case.

22 Does the punning increase your enjoyment of the play, or do you think that it is overdone? Which persons of the play indulge in it most?

23 Give three or four examples of dramatic irony from the play, and explain fully wherein the dramatic irony consists.

24 Which part in the play would you most like to act? Which do you think is the most difficult part to act? In each case give your reasons.

25 Describe an imaginary visit to an Elizabethan theatre for a performance of *Twelfth Night*.